The Red Bird Sings at Night

The Red Bird Sings at Night

A collection of poems about trauma, mental illness, and self-transformation

Melissa Guenther

Dedication

To anyone out there who is struggling, who feels alone, hopeless or misunderstood; this is for you.

You matter so much more than you think and you can get past these feelings; whatever darkness and hopelessness you're holding inside. **This painful period of your life will one day be the story of your triumphs.** Mental illness is hard, it can't be seen and it makes it difficult to understand and accept.

I also would like to dedicate this book to all those that have helped me when I couldn't help myself. To those that saw me when I couldn't remember who that was anymore. For the unconditional love I received despite my mistakes. To everyone that picked me up when my legs were too heavy and to everyone that was compassionate enough to sit in the dark with me.

Thank You From the Bottom of My Heart

Author's Note

During my late adolescence, I began having intense feelings of Borderline Personality Disorder; unbeknownst to me for years to come, it steadily grew worse. During that time in my life my perception, emotional stability and control began to plummet. I battled a severe mental illness I had no insight or knowledge of. I began to sink in all areas of my life until I couldn't ignore it anymore. Saving myself became my only focus. Learning how to stay alive became my sole priority.

As my life and mind began to unravel, more labels appeared, more answers; labels like *Bipolar*, and *PTSD*. It took weeks of lifelessness; months of isolation and crying in bed. *Years* of confusion and determination for truth and healing; years of draughts in my writing, until I was finally able find my way back to myself. My life became an endless journey to find forgiveness in those that caused me trauma; and most of all, being able to find forgiveness with *myself*. Forgiveness is the best way to find healing. It's critical. Resentment and anger prevent us from feeling better and letting go of pain; whether it's directed at someone or ourselves. When we learn to let go, we learn how to be free again. We allow our hearts to lighten their load.

Ernest Hemingway once said "Write hard and clear about what hurts." I found solace in these words, in my notebooks and the words that flowed from my hand; taking me away from the confusion of my life, the actions I could not understand and the hopelessness and emptiness I felt.

When stability began to return to my mind, when clear thinking and self-control came back again; I began to purge all that pain. Pain I felt guilty to talk about, pain I ignored for the sake of others; all that I had bottled in for most of my life. The pains of my past, regrets I have to live with, mistakes I can't go back to, mistreatment I can't undo; the tornado that concocts the mind of Borderline Personality Disorder.

I never thought healing was possible, but I couldn't have been further from the truth.

Healing is possible once you are ready to face yourself.

These words, these poems, poured from my heart as I thought about my past, the experiences that shaped me, and the pain within and around me. As I began finally getting the help and support I needed, I started writing again. I began utilizing that writing, and my journaling, to better understand myself, my illness and my past, and those that have harmed me. Writing became a conduit for me to face the many truths of my life.

This book is my truth, my trauma and my mistakes. Openly and honestly. It's me finding closure with my toxic past and the dysfunction I grew up in and created. Most importantly, I want to help those with mental illness to know there is healing, the whirlwind you might be living in or feel inside, is normal and you can find peace and stability again. I want anyone out there who struggles with their mental health to understand **there is no shame**. Your struggles are no different from a physical illness; take care of yourself and do not be afraid to ask for help. You matter, time heals all wounds and mistakes; you are not broken, and you are loved. If not by someone, by me. Whether you know me or not I have endless love and compassion for those who keep fighting, to the survivors and the brave souls who have unrelenting strength to keep moving forward. Everything about you, good and bad, is what makes you uniquely you. Thank you for being here, **you are beautiful and you are amazing.**

Contents

Trigger Warning

I never want anyone to be accosted with triggering thoughts, topics, or actions. I want to note that in my choice to be honest about the realities of the good and bad of my disorders and my healing journey there are heavy topics illustrated and mentioned. Topics can include: truths of metal illnesses, self-harm, suicidal ideation, disordered eating, poor coping mechanisms, abuse, PTSD, and trauma.

Please, if at any point you feel triggered or affected by any of these topics, take a step back, it is okay to not feel okay. It's okay to react strongly to heavy topics, be kind to yourself.

"Everything heals. Your body heals. Your heart heals. The mind heals. Wounds heal. Your soul repairs itself. Your happiness is always going to come back"

~ Christiana Rutkowski

Innocence Part One

"No man knows the value of innocence and integrity but he who has lost them"

\-   William Godwin

Little Doe

Little Doe
You can't find safety with a hunter
Don't you know?

Run

  Hide

    Be safe

Don't fall into the chase…

The more you look nearer
The easier you become clearer
He's only planning to get a taste
A helpless soul he can poison and erase

You feel the danger
But you creep forward, taking the chance
Bravery fueled by youthful overconfidence

He stands ready
Hands very steady

You realize it's too late
Your curiosity will be your fate

Lips dripping with desire
A weak prey ready for the slaughter

You stand frozen, with eyes screaming
horror
The hunter smiles, with eyes of fire

Your heart stops
A silent tear drops
The predator remains on top
Ruthless, heartless, with an unheard cry
Little doe pleads why
With a bang and a drop
It's too late to save her
But that's what she gets
For trusting in the smooth stranger

Witness

Eyes that would be better off blind
Actions that confused and tormented my
mind

Evil and rage
Superiority constantly engaged
Bruises I saw
Constant actions without law

A serpent in public
Telling stories to the republic
Comfortably walking their stage
Naive eyes to engage

But my eyes were witnesses
To countless instances
I heard every cry
I was small
But I knew why

The House That I Know

Rooms that breathe secrets
Memories of regrets
Photographs with piercing eyes
No safety here, too many spies

Hallowed walls
Empty halls
A house ready to fall
Give it up, take it all

Bruises on my heart
That weren't there from the start
A taint under my skin
That slithered its way in

A sickness
A poison
I drink to impress
I smile, I swallow, accepting the mess

It pleases them
I've passed the test
I cough up the phlegm
Getting ready to rest

The light is fading
The dark is taking
The windows are closed
The night has arose

The wolf howls
The dark conceals the days fouls
Teeth bared, the wolf rises
Facing all he despises

The pain spreads
The wolf holds on by threads
Still relentlessly coming for your head
The wolf won't stop until its prey is dead

Forced Confrontations

Pinned
And so it begins

Trapped
Suffocating beneath the pressure

Get off of me
I just want to breathe

I'm innocent, I swear
I have nothing to share

I'm only six, but I'm not a liar
I promise, I think there's no fire

I just want to play
Please protect me and take me away

I can't admit to what I don't know
I can't present what you want me to show

I'm sorry
You know as much as me
Can I please just be a kid
Let me be free

Police with Eyes of Shame

Every time they come
Chaos has already begun

Always too late
Actions have already found their fate

They sift through the bullshit
Acts and terrible lies
While their view drifts
To two small, wounded eyes

A pang of shame
A momentary flash

Sorrow they cannot hide
For the children trapped inside

Consolation Prize

It's not about love
It's not about care

It can't be seen
But it's plainly there

Hearts that are infected
While everyone's affected
Blinded and selfish

A moment that's lost all joy
Arguing over their helpless little toy

Short-sighted by desire
Not caring what they destroy
A power struggle fueled in fire
Forgetting their toy

It hangs on by a thread
Yanking and pulling
One last merciless tug
And it's off with its head
The toy is gone
Its soul is dead

Who

Dysfunction and violence
Scary nights of silence
A childhood of destitute

Screaming and yelling
Making myself small
Avoiding the adults, avoiding them all
Always the perpetrator
The liar and evader

Raised to feel vile
Escape futile
Life became my betrayer
Say a prayer for me
Save your hate for later

Crushed by their inquisitions
Put in the middle of horrid lies
Who did what, superstitions
Despite my pleas and cries

Hope deteriorated by the life I had
befallen
A mind aged
A childhood stolen
Adapting, changing my ways
Always much wiser than my days

Counselors appearing

DYFYS domineering
Stress and prodding
Feeding into what everyone was fearing
Judgmental looks, sweet kind nodding

Innocence
Stole by lack of common sense
A ruthless divorce
A sheep slaughtered
A life headed for a painful course

Zero remorse
For the trauma
The drama
And the lies you so easily endorsed

Heartless
Selfish
Anything to win the game
Ready to concoct a story, to throw blame
Anything to get your way
A cruel victory, you'd continue to relish
No matter the tyranny, or the lives you
made hellish

Plans that crumbled
Your sick strategy fumbled
Rage at your failed play
Harassing the child, but begging her to stay
Like a possession, an object wasting away

No choice, no visibility, no say

Monster House

Controlling
Eyes constantly patrolling
The monster relishing in its power
Eyes filled with glee
With every passing hour
What is wrong with me?

Constant anxiety
A home I wanted to flee
Ridiculed and humiliated
Despicable things you related
The home we all hated
The resentment and lies
The child you despised

Too small to be believed
Justified was the shame I received
Silenced
Ignored
Neglected
Raised in a home where I felt rejected

What should've been my safety
Became the stress I carried daily
While the monster strut around
triumphantly

They made me believe I had no use
It wasn't until I became a teen

That anger could face abuse
And mean face mean

Your crown tumbled hard
A home you were barred
Kicked from the castle
Trailed by scars
Finally taking back what's ours

Peace

Sweet release

Goodbye monster

Goodbye beast

What I Know

Some girls daydreamed of a knight to
rescue them
Of grand weddings
And beautiful gowns
Of babies
Tumbling around

But me
Determined little I
Beneath what anyone could see

All I ever wanted
Was to buy a home
A place I could call my own

Where warmth pours
Like light streams through glass doors

Where love is abundant
An unconditional force
A primary source

Where voices are low and persecution dies
An honest place, empty of lies

A peaceful place
I don't wish to erase
Somewhere to go
When I'm lost in space

Consistency and stability
Every night I close my eyes
No longer surrounded by those I despise

Rest and reprise

Pieces

I don't remember a lot of things
But I remember that house

I don't remember a lot of things
But I remember that room

I don't remember a lot of things
But I remember that closet

The one where we hid
After what he had did

–

I can still hear the cries
Within his home of lies

I can still see the bruises
But not the hit

But I guess that was her fault
She tried to stop it

–

I don't remember a lot of things
That were clearly worth remembering

What I couldn't remember
Blindly branded me

Until my eyes could finally see
All the damage done
To an obvious casualty

Too innocent to understand
Trapped in the tornado
Waiting to be free
Not understanding anything more
Than wanting to flee

There's a lot I don't remember
As much as I try
So many holes

I just want to know why
Why they all would lie
About what I don't remember
Take me back
I need to know

You might think we've left
You might think it's all gone
But in my mind
That house lives on

Intergenerational Trauma

I can't blame you dad
It's okay mama
I know it's been hard
I know you have trauma

You did the best with what you knew
I no longer spend time blaming you

I will do whatever I need to do
To heal in me, what you couldn't heal in you

So that my children
Know something different

Innocence Part Two

"The trust of the innocent is the liars most useful tool"

\-   Stephen King

Sweet Peach
She had auburn hair
And olive tinged skin
Hair a fiery blaze
Foreshadowing a powerful force within

A gypsy soul
With the heart of a hippy
She'll love you hard
Before chasing a new city

Eyes a deep brown
That change with the sun
A wild soul on the run
Sweet little peach
She's always out of reach

How I Know
I either melt
Or I don't

My eyes either dart
Or pass over

My heart either jumps
Or feels nothing

There is no changing
It cannot be undone
It's simply instinctive

Something New
Words are just words,
  Until
    they
      come
          from
            you
The sky is just blue,
  Until
    I
      stare
        longingly
            with
              you
Music is the same,
  Until
    we're
      dancing
        in
              the
                rain
Love was just love,
  Until
    you
      were
        sent
            from
              above

Old Soul

Old soul
You whispered to me
With wounded eyes
That could truly see

A depth hidden among what's shallow

Innocent Girl

They forget to mention
My dear
That without closer inspection
Bad guys look and sound
A hell of a lot like good guys

The only difference
Is seeing through their lies

Need

Hand outstretched
A soul to feed
A love you wanted to become a need

Sneaky

Your hands on my body
Is my new favorite hobby

Sneaky sexts
Wondering what's next

A distraction to hold together
The remnants of my soul
Needing to feel
For even one second
Loved and whole

You know
You know
Which is why you never go

Greedy souls in need
Broken and starved
Ready to feed

Selfless pasts shed
From the compassions that made us dead

Swimming

Lost but often found
Eyes like yours
Spinning me around

The scent of your cologne still lingers
Another night of danger
In your slumber you pull me closer
Nuzzling your head into the crook of my
shoulder
Forgotten are the moments you would
hold her

You twist your body
Molding every inch firm
Against the curves of me
Lost individuality
Nothing but a bodily mass for all to see

A sigh of relief
A moment of reprieve
A mind allowed to finally breathe

Brown tuffs of hair
Draped delicately across your face
Eyes full of love
No hatred can ever erase

The smell of roses wafting through the air
I trail my fingers over the silk of your skin
Daring your dreams to let me in

Fingers down your spine
Sweet kisses, lost time

Your lips are near
I can feel you here
The warmth of your breath
Against the tip of my ear
There's nothing to fear
Enveloped in your safety my dear

Wrapped in heaven
Clock barely reaching eleven
Hours to go
What's to come, nobody knows
Before you go
With the closing of a door
With a sighing breath
And a quiet snore

Blind

Eyes that glitter
A heart that's swooning
Craving safety
Unknown
Is the danger looming
An innocent soul
You're heartlessly dooming

So subtle
Of course
So there will be no rebuttal

Manipulating
A mind you're desecrating
Loving someone
I should be hating

Legendary
Eyes filled with love
Hidden away
Carried by the words
Of Fitzgerald
Plath
And Hemingway

The words I want to say
The eloquent way they convey
The storms of the heart
Of this life
And things that fall apart

Soul Kiss
There's just something
In the way he calls my soul beautiful

Sweet Melody
Loving you
Made music
From the silence
Of my dying heart

Moments Like This
Sitting by the bay
Massages while we lay
Hours that pass
Slow like days
While the rest of the world fades away

With You

Sex with you
Is always something new
Oh the things we would do

Eyes black with desire
Instinct burning the internal fire
Souls possessed
Minds obsessed

Bodies made for one another
Sex like no other

The things we knew
The appearances we would misconstrue
While nobody had a clue

Our moments together
Deep pleasure
Giving and giving
Dominating
And hating

A game of cat and mouse
While you flipped me around this house

Teasing and testing
Conniving and provoking
With a giggle and a toss
A face off with the boss

Moments that can't be breached
Intensity that can't be reached
Without a little crazy

Complimentary
Serenity
Wild child
Scorpio queen
Angel and devil
Innocent and mean

Lines that can get a little hazy
Don't stop, fuck me baby

Elevated
Your love is my favorite high
If I could overdose
I'd choose to die

Falling Star

I never said we weren't doomed
I'm not that naive
There's a lot a smile can achieve

But who says we can't chance the weather
And implode together?

Loss

My love
I can see the sadness in your eyes
My love
I hear your silent cries
Hold on
My wounded swan
I know you just want to be gone

My sweet
I know the world looks like it's ending
My sweet
I know your strengths past pretending
Behind the masks, your souls been beat
My sweet
This is pain
But not defeat

My dear
This is life
My dear
There are many strifes
Life was made for many more
Cheers, jeers
And blubbering tears

Baby
I will carry you
When the days turn blue
I will hold you

If this love is true
If I mean
What you do
You will never face this pain alone
You know these two arms will always be
home

The Basics

Loyalty
Honesty
And compassion

Support
Love
And protection

Who knew one day
These would be the traits
That I would beg for and pray
Hoping they were true
And ready to stay

We All Know One

He'll feed you hope
On a silver platter
Knowing his words
Will be all that will matter

It's a lie
It's a lie

Save yourself the heartache
Abuse
And misuse

Just say goodbye
One day you'll understand why

Of Course

The devil wears
The most handsome smile
Or you wouldn't
Stay for a while

The Mark of The Devil

Possessive
And
Oppressive

And So It Goes

One minute
They are the
Words in every
Song

The next
They are
All things
That could've gone wrong

Missing the Bliss

Ignorance was so sweet to me

Vanishing Aura

Drained by what gives me life
A spiritual sacrifice
An aura that's fading
Magic that's depleting

Reaching for what
I cannot fulfill
With my last dying will

Energy lost
Malnourished of creative strength
Soul food she's been starved
While buried in the dark
With eyes shut
And hands frozen
She is an artist
That can no longer exist

47   The Red Bird Sings at Night

Interdependence Part Three

"Ignorance speaks loudly, so as to be heard; but its volume proves reason to doubt every word"

- Wes Fessler

In Love with a Stranger

Danger
Danger
I'm in love with a stranger

He's stolen my heart
He's ripping me apart

Lost in his eyes
Fucked by his lies
When his breath is near
My body knows no fear

A love that fiends
Only witnessed in dreams
I'm ready for a dose
Fill me up
Baby pull me close

Nuzzling my skin
Begging me
To let you in

Whoever you are
When we are apart
Is a stranger to me
Is someone I don't know
And will never see

But here

Right now
We lay in ecstasy
Alone in the dark
Content somehow

A safe place
Where time stands still
We take up no space
Hidden in the world of shadows
Listening to the silence
Of the worlds echoes

Irresistible

Your outline
Pressed against my spine
Always running out of time

Fire and ice
Passion and desire

Tossing a match
Without expecting a fire

Quick witted
A sharp mind
Two warm bodies, tightly entwined

Dangerous
You and I
Drowning with every lie
Sacrificing
And expecting not to die

Lies as Sweet as Pie

He coated abuse
With sugary lips

Please Stop

You take the life out of my days
When you remain
In your toxic ways

Futility

Lessons learned
From the constant burns
Mistakes my mind can't eliminate
Truth I can't discriminate

Abuse
    and
        Misuse

Mental strain
Is all that will remain

No escape
Always the same fate

Gone

Take me away
My mind is lost
This heart will never defrost
Stop pushing me
Then begging me to stay

How Many?

How many other women
Did you take by the water
Is that how you'd want them
To treat your daughter?

How many women
Did you venture to the village?

How many women
Did you sell your story?
Only caring
About the ending glory

How many innocent girls
Stayed up late
Stargazing on *your* first date?

The House You Burnt to The Ground

Seduced by the demon
Controlled by what does not please him
Locked away
Brainwashed to stay
A soul buried by the betrayal and disarray

In her darkest hour
When life turned sour
A light in the dark
A fake reality
A possessive mark

Layers
Stripped like paint
Peeled the wallpapers
From where she laid ready to faint

Trauma exposed, the most vile act
The abuser spews lies, never fact
Overwhelmed
Overtaken
By thoughts of things forsaken
Brain shaking
From the truth that you were taking

Skin burned from the trails of your touch
A bed that becomes an escape
When the pain is too much

Emptiness
Mind shook
From all the things you showed me
Every lie, all that you took

Thoughts that cry
The never ending stress
Strength that's daily put to test
Plagued by unrelenting distress
Fueled by the resentment and anger I'd
ingest

The never ending darkness
The nights filled with starkness
Done with fake romance
Tired of this sad little dance

Lost and fallen
Shattered trust that she had befallen
She lay there, mind reeling
Hugged by sheets, trying to find healing
From all the bullshit that he was revealing

True colors shed
Love like the walls that run red
All the things you had said
That made everyone want to be dead

Chipped paint
A heart that's been stolen
Dreary faded walls

A mind broken
From the nonsense
The words that you had spoken

A line crossed
Respect tossed
An end chosen
A home that's been burned
Relationships frozen

Experimental

Intentions fabricated
By a dark haze
A mouse
Trapped in his maze
Eyes locked
An unwavering gaze

Lips that smile
Before they take a bite
No soul left to fight
Draining you
A life turned blue

He poisoned me
While simultaneously
Keeping me alive
Kill and revive

Dissecting my mind
Searching for what he cannot find
Projected mistrust
Controlling
No matter how unjust

Open heart surgery
Searching for disloyalty
Plagued by fears
Of endless treachery

Will depleting
While my heart keeps beating
A body that's bleeding
While he keeps feeding

Prince Charming
Gaslight
Gaslight
Anything
        to
            win
                a
                    fight

Eyes that despise
Lies you comprise
Slow defense
Raging offense

A roach in my home
A memory I can't kill
Love that's lost its thrill
Manipulation
Infestation

You were
All I could see
That's how I let you
Take advantage of me

You lead me when I was blind
But now I can't unsee
Everything that's been
Right in front of me

Explosive
You
And
I

Impossible to deny

Nagasaki

Fukushima

Cataclysmic
You and me

Two disasters
Ready for all to see

Deep in feelings
Lost in the cloud

Angry
    and
        loud

The dark swallows the nights' cries
Hope ends the vicious lies
The sun will soon rise
As we begin our free fall
Plummeting to our demise

The Pot that Calls the Kettle Black

Witch
He cries
To bury her honesty with lies

Banking on deflection
Of those he shows affection

His only protection
Within the web of his deception
His only defense is projection
And angry deflection

The Cycle

Back into the abyss
Where love has run amiss

Music has run dry
My ears have lost sound
I feel you here but no one's around

My mind keeps spinning
Turning me around

Lost is the fantasy
Forgotten is the reality

A love we devour
When it's sweet and when it's sour

Taking me high
Elevated by your every lie

Before I'm crashing as I'm descending
Always our fated ending

Only You

Lost in an anxiety induced daze
Insides ablaze
Mind reeling
Only you
Can cause this feeling

Tendons slither beneath my skin
My chest seizes
My will is thin

Righteous paranoia
A mind full of diseases

Nerve endings burning alive
Fighting to survive

Self-worth lost all meaning
From internal pain
And actions without restrain
Warmth overtaken by icy cold
Strength ready to fold

Tightening
     Twisting
A fist around my heart
      Squeezing
        Suffocating
Beating it quicker

Slow death
A feeling I've never felt before
Fear with every shallow breath
Who knows what else is in store

Terror
Panic
Distress
Constantly a mess

Let me go
Please stay

I hate you
Please be better

You're worthless
I need you

An ache without you
Silently oppressed

Miserable and blue
Constant unrest

Kicking you out
Panicking in protest

Only you

Only you

Could do what you do

But you already know that

Isn't that true?

No Shades of Grey
Memories that stand still
Nights of fights and broken will
Words with air
But meaning not there

There's a hole in my chest
I can feel it expanding
Every second we go on pretending
I breathe, I try, I do my best

                    Over

            Ove

        Ov

O

        Ov

            Ove

                Over

The word echoes around the cavern of my
mind
Panic, anxiety, thoughts of leaving you
behind
In a void filled with nothing but remnants
of you

In what reality can this be true?

What happened to forever
That resilience that screamed never?
Unbreakable, impenetrable
Shattered from the inside
Dishonorable
No longer anywhere to hide
Actions without love, hate chosen to divide

My love, my last dying light
How can I forget the man from that night?
Who pulled me close and held me tight
When I didn't get it just right

He kissed my scars
Absorbed the salt of my tears
Took me to see the stars
And rid me of my fears

Hidden beneath the shade of the tree
His love ate away the darkness
The hole inside of me
Overpowered by what he forced me to see
A future filled with love
A peaceful eternity
My sweet
My loving dove

The silence of the night

The stillness of the moment
Years of pain repressed
Faults my mind obsessed

Darkness he knew
Before we ever dated
Discarded respect
Mistakes we both hated

Tenderly he held me
Cradling my face
Counting my breaths
While my mind entered space
Distracting the mania
Plummeting back to Earth
A cosmic rebirth
Rescuing my soul
From a deep black hole

He was what I needed
Now I'm just defeated
Trust he destroyed
Emotions he toyed
Pushing me away
Until I could no longer stay

The frontlines of Mental warfare
Admission to the battle
First to embark
Into the unknown of the dark

Confusion, illness, a brain that felt rattled
Two broken hearts utterly baffled

Uncontrollable, explosive
In a relationship that's corrosive
Disassociation
Generalization
Over stimulation
A heart on vacation

I'm sorry

I'm sorry

Borderline
Will always be my crime

I love you

I hate you

Please understand
Everything makes sense again when you
take my hand

Don't go
There's no deeper sorrow
My heart depletes with every hour
Every second closer to tomorrow

Lifeless

My veins drip you out
Like a drug I bleed you dry
Distorted, another high
Craving, as the drops start thinning
Empty, a new world beginning

When It Was Over
Life lost its color
Everything took on a dark hue

Music lost its sound
The sky lost its blue

Happiness wasn't the same anymore
TV shows, movies, books
Nothing appears as it looks

Nothing is the same anymore

Not since you walked through the door
And not after you left looking for more

Cutting Ties

What will happen
With time and space?
Will you take our memories
Click delete and erase?
Will you stop caring
If you see my face?

'What ifs' plague me
Poison and break me

Because every minute you slip away
My heart continues a slow decay
I wish with my whole being
You'd simply stay

I know you want to get better
I know it's harder together
But I'd still choose to chance the weather
Holding deeply to our strong tether

Not cut the ties
A choice you knew I'd despise
NEVER
Did I expect you'd choose to sever

Gone

The phone doesn't ring
Silence just sings
From the absence
Of all that you'd bring

Alone

Perpetually
I opened my soul for you
Now again I'm closed
Like a flower past season
No longer able to find reason

There's a void inside
While I'm trapped
In this life I must reside
With a will that's gone
And a heart that's died
You said you'd be here forever
But you lied

Justified
In your mind
Something better left behind
I just wish you had another answer
Something less painful to find

Fabricated

Notoriety
Fueled by lost sobriety

False memories
Truths formulated
From the lies they related

Trusting in snakes
You'll get a juicy story
What once was sweet, they turned whorey

Exaggerations
Are their favorite relations

Don't believe every word that's said
Or your mind will stay active
While sense is left for dead

You Know
I never needed you
But your power was making me
Feel like I do

The Ghosts We See

I was in love
With a memory
That had long left me

A Horrid Kind of Character

What it must be like
To live guilt free
To have the arrogance of peace of mind
Regardless of the destruction you left
behind

Your castle is crumbling
Your actions are fumbling
Your crown is tumbling

Lies that have woven so deep
Stories you can no longer upkeep
This is what you chose to sow
Now live with what you reap

Emotional Torment

A
liar

and

a

cheater

You were abusive

Even
if
you
did
not
beat
her

Skeletons

Skeletons in my closet
I wish I could let out

Beating at the door
They want to explore

Set us free!
Set us free!

I can hear their shouts

Monster!
Monster!

It is I no doubt

I sit beside them
While they sit inside of me

I can feel their clawing
I hear the clanking of their bones

Pounding and screaming to be
Let out, open and free

Moaning
And
Groaning

Scratching

And
Chipping

Their strength and numbers
Not worth resisting
No longer can I control them
Or cease remembering

My ears bleed
Trying to run from what they need
My heart knows no home
It's a battle I deserve
To face alone

There's no longer anyone to blame
Just learning to live with the shame
That I became
The most dangerous adversary
To me

In the Eye of the Storm
I am a nuke
When I am done

My chest is fire
My heart is destruction
My minds facing abduction
Soul lost by the darkness's suction

Fuck the rain
I am a hurricane

Walls That Tell Stories
Blue

Calm and innocent
Before any of you
And my tailspin into descent

Red

Passion, fire, anger
I started playing with danger
I believed every word you said
Despite the warnings inside my head

Grey

Empty, lost, broken
My heart started to fade away
Running from the lies you spoke
The apologies you'd revoke
Suffocating on the words you'd choke

Fumbling over your excuses
Fights, gas lighting, completely useless

In blindness and clarity
We both knew it was time to flee

I'll paint my walls and forget you
The memories, the pain and the falls
The cries, late nights, your drunken calls

All the darkness that hid there
A new comfort to share
As if you weren't ever there

Imbalance

Part Four

"To live is to suffer, to survive is to find some meaning in the suffering"

\-   Friedrich Nietzsche

The Darkest Night
The sun will not rise
Say your goodbyes

The end is near
The darkness is here

Let go

Free fall
Give it up
Take it all

Disconnected

Disappointed

Futile
And
Pointless

Wanting love
Finding hate
A confusion most can relate

Wanting to be famous
Ending up nameless

A dreamer
With no sight

A bird
With clipped wings

A home empty
But filled with things

A day
Fading away

Instability
Nothing feels okay

My hope is depleting
My will is bleeding
The night is winning
My light is dwindling

Clawing my way to tomorrow
With a heart weighted in sorrow
I want to survive
Please keep me alive

Instability
Earthquake
Loss of footing
The ground is missing
Everything's slipping

Disorienting
Sinking
No time for thinking
Pain
Pain
Pain
The only thing that will remain

Spinning
This is it
Falling
Into the dark
Lost
The end is near

Finally

I made it
I am here

In a Parallel Universe

My parents would be together

My family would be loving

My home would be kind

My boyfriends would be good to me

My mind a chemical balance

My future clear

A life with abundant happiness

Anything but this...

Cold

When you grow up with beasts
The feel of the claw
Doesn't sting quite the same

Chemicals
Oxytocin
Serotonin
Dopamine
Endorphins

Take your pick
When they change
Your brain reacts real quick

Splitting

Day by day
Taunting you
And begging you to stay
A game you never agreed to play

Praising you
Putting you on a pedestal
Right now you can do no wrong
You are my safety all day long

Until the splitting begins
When nobody wins
Like the spark of a bomb
I'm set off
I **hate** you
I think it's true?

Degrading one minute
Too lost in it
To put on the breaks
Before crashing chaotically
And ruminating on my mistakes

Delusional
You were someone else
You were my enemy
A perpetrator was all I could see
Yet this loving man
Was still standing right in front of me
How can that be?

I don't understand
It felt so real
How will I ever go back
To trusting how I feel?

Cognitive Distortions
Perception and reality
Don't always agree

It might seem okay to you
But horrible to me

Dysfunctional thoughts
Powerful onslaughts

A twisted reality
A broken symphony

Unable to trust
The brain inside my head
That sooner wishes me dead

I'm hostage
To my own self sabotage

Comorbidity
Borderline
Bipolar
Depression
Anxiety
PTSD
Binge Eater

What more can I take?
How many more labels will they make?

Hypervigilant

A life sentence
A dreary penance
For crimes I have no remembrance

Sensitivity
The symptoms of a casualty

No one can see
Or understand the distress inside me

High Functioning

Everything is too much

I didn't ask for this life
As selfish as it sounds

I just want to be alone
To heal and atone

I need help, there's no way to coat it
The hard workers can break too
The survivors can crack
We're all under constant attack

Your expectations of me
Are drowning me
All these roles
I'm expected to fulfill
While I'm slowly dying on top of this hill

I look like I'm good
I look like I'm fine
Yes I'm maintaining
But I'm slowly losing my mind

This world is exhausting
I'm struggling to breathe
Begging you to notice
How much I need a reprieve

My strength is slipping

I'm losing my will
Everything's changing
While I stand still
Never ending demands
I'm expected to fulfill

I'm so close to caving
Please help me while I'm still worth saving

Holes

There are so many holes
Gaps in my memories

Blocked trauma
Forgotten terror and drama

No One

My pain is life or death
Every struggle puts my will power to the
test
My life is a mess

Please save me
End this god damn broken melody

Physical

Trying to get out of my head
Focusing on the breath instead

Tightness in my chest
An internal sickness
A mind unable to rest
A pain my body detests

Save me
From this invisible enemy
My brain is my biggest adversary
Worry after worry
Thoughts I can't help but implore
The darkness I'm forced to explore

Left
  Defenseless

To torture
  That's
    Endless

Somebody
  End
    This

These Pessimistic Eyes

A series of unfortunate events
That's what the culmination of my life
represents

The Luck of the Draw

6 of us
But only madness running inside of me?
How can that be?

Often My Illness

I'm too high when I'm lazy

Why
One word
Endless torture

The Human Condition

Doomed to be human
Doomed to cease to exist
Vanishing one day
Like the passing of mist

A life filled with yearning
Of things we can't resist
One day to suffer
For all that we miss

Plagued by the signs and symptoms of time
Doomed to age
Doomed to break
A life we will one day forsake

While most go through
Being nothing but fake
Worrying about
All they can take

Doomed to fall in love
To feel so high
Yet come to a crushing low
Suffering blow after blow

Doomed to lose all that we cherish
To see our families slip away
While we continue our own decay

What is the point?

It's all temporary
Destiny my friends
Is very scary

Internal Snapping

Like a rubber band
I can snap
From one direction
To the next
Debilitating to you
Overwhelming to me
A darkness I can't flea
Breaking when no one can see

Happy one moment
Genuine, pleasant
Comfortable and content

Then it happens
My mind begins its race
Pain it wants to continue to chase

The beginning of a dark descent
Sinking
Smiling
A brain I furiously resent
Eyes that keep blinking
Over drinking
Innocent for you
Destructive to me
While you blindly joke with joyful glee

No signs

Just an internal stinger

Thoughts that linger
Pulling the trigger

No exceptions
Despite the height of my love
I warned you
I didn't come from above

A mind fueling internal oppression
Controlled by my demons
A spirit that's become a possession
Something to chase
To distract from what cannot be erased

With a single flick
Here one minute
Then gone so quick

Addicted to my love

Hair burning red like a beacon
Daring you closer
To come explore
Seductive eyes that lore
To the dangers of my shore

I should've gave a warning
About my siren call
As soon as you come near
You've already lost it all

A heart that has no sway
A craving you can't delay
Desire no word could satisfy
An urge that must be rectified
What started as desire became reality
With every passing moment of lost
morality

Like a drug
You let me in
Warm, sweet and snug
Relishing in sin
Sweet whispers
Claws that dug

A love you never meant to find
Seeping through

your body

Your soul

Your mind

A love you gladly followed blind

Come closer my sweet
Close your eyes
It's okay to stay
Forget the pain and sorrows of yesterday
You no longer have to fear the lies

The loneliness

and

silent goodbyes

You've reached my shores
My heart is forever yours
When it shines and when it pours

BPD Has Got a Hold on Me

I know
It's killing me
But I don't stop

I live in the pain
Ruminate in its toxicity
The penance I deserve
For my past disruptions
Explosions
And eruptions

Aggression
Is my new obsession
A masochist
In endless depression

Venom running through my veins
I know he's killing me
But I don't stop him

What the Neighbors See

I can only imagine what my neighbors
think
Listening to my downfall, hearing me sink
A mental collapse, always on the brink

Screaming my throat raw
Exposing my wrong doings
I can only wonder what they heard
And all that they saw

I'm more than this turmoil
I'm more than my crimes
It goes so much deeper than these little
rhymes

I lost my sanity
Because of a shattered reality
I was a casualty
Adrift at sea
I needed someone to save me

Not knowing it was my job
All the time I would rob
Of my personal healing
While I'd curl up and sob

Easy

Sad poems are easy
Pain comes in so many flavors

But happiness

Happiness has a stronger taste

Drowning
Sinking and thinking
Thinking and sinking

The Puppeteer of the Blind

Words that drip like acid
To a heart that's placid
I sit back and smile
Absorbing it for a while

They think they're sneaky
They think they're kind
They think I don't know
About the whispers when I go

The silent puppeteer
To the snakes hiding near
Lost little puppets
I pull the strings
Knowing the horror it brings

Sticks and stones
I laugh untouched
Conniving just a little too much

Stirring the pot
Misleading the blind
Black hearts, with bitter minds
Their lives breaking from the seams, days
falling apart
Transparent to everyone from the start

Watch your back if you enter this garden
Before my heart completely hardens

Ruthless, don't tempt me
It's easy to fight, when you feel empty

You think the fun has just begun
But sweetheart the games already been
won

Fluctuations

Binging my emotions
Swallowing them whole

RAVENOUS
Like an animal

Eating myself into a slumber
Fearing the scale
And its increasing number

Measuring my wrist
Assessing my waist
Fasting for days
A determination that stays

Zero desire
No matter how dire
Craving no taste
Curves and folds
I'd kill to erase
Not wanting to take up any space

A weight that constantly fluctuates
Healthy one minute
Bordering anorexic the next
Never knowing what to expect

Proud of the bones that begin to protrude
Struggling everyday with my food

What should bring me sustenance
I see only consequence
A dreary penance
Towards a body I hate
Never knowing
If this will be my fate

The Mind of a Masochist
I keep scissors in my bed
To scare all the monsters inside my head

'I have scissors' I had said
'For moments when I'm feeling dead'

I have scissors in my hand
Wondering when they'll understand
Understand

I feel scissors on my skin
Let them in, let them in

I have scissors that left scars
Glossy white, like the stars

I see scissors in my nightmares
Lying near my body
Skin soaked by tears
Trapped by their unknowing stares
Plagued by unrelenting fears

Fading

Evading

Disintegrating

Dying a nobody, by becoming somebody

The Kiss of the Blade

It's never a snap decision
It's never about anyone else
It's about a hatred I harbor over myself

An internal resentment
At my lack of coping
At who I am at my core
And the emptiness I'm too afraid to
explore

The scars are growing
There's no room to hide
Soon they'll all see
There's a monster inside

It's no ones fault but mine
But that won't stop this twisted mind
From hurling blame
And hating you by name
While I sink in shame

Committed

Drugged and dazed
Waking up
From a foggy haze
Delirious and lost
Are a few of my days

Rigid beds and sterile walls
A miserable little place
An unescapable maze
Everyone clawing to get out
In a destined race

Panic stricken in a foreign place
Betrayed and abandoned
You'd never understand
I was left alone
In enemy land

Surrounded by broken souls
Chaos, violence, and constant fights
I can't get out, I've lost my rights

Take these pills
Here's your cup
Swallow and cough
Try not to erupt

Searching out windows
Any chance I could get
Trying to keep my cool

Trying not to get upset

Dropped in a snow globe
Cold and wet
White as far as the eye could see
Trees lining the distance
Pointless is my resistance
Somebody save me
I'm surrounded
My mind is confounded

Relying on strangers
To keep me from the dangers
Trapped in lines
Never ending hours
And early bedtimes

Groups shuffle me along
Crafts keep me distracted
Socializing
Finding others with minds like mine
Is all I can do to satisfy my time

Limping from table to table
I make friends with my jokes
Who would've thought
I'd get along so well with these folks

They're not depraved, vile, or rotten
They're not worth being forgotten
They're kind, empathetic, and broken

But unfortunately people judge them
Before they've ever even spoken

I learned a lot in my time here
Regardless of my rage, disdain, or fear
I gained a perspective of humans
Of myself and my demons
Something that I hope forever remains

They locked me up
But they didn't throw away the key
I wasn't as hopeless as I thought I would be
I was more than what everyone could see
Now and forever more,
I am free.

Drainage
                        in the shower
sunken

A day or an hour
Broken
Shattered
A heart that's splattered

D
   r
      a
        i
      n
        i
      n
        g

My life slips away
S   i   l   e   n   c   e
Letting the water devour
Shedd
    i
       n
       g
All things bleak and sour

Thoughts that Stick

Happy thoughts
Don't hit quite the same

Dismissed
By a mentally ill brain

Fighting
For each day

Smiling
Despite my hearts dismay

Moving
Towards a better day

Praying
To simply hear "it's okay"

BPD vs Therapy
Dismissal
Denial
Swimming in the Nile
Of over self confidence
Convincing myself for a little while

Screaming
Destructive
Need surpassed by a last resort

Vanishing
Gone
No longer a snide retort

Trauma Responses

Disassociation
Deflection
Defenses
and aggression

I assure you if it's fight or flight
I don't care whose wrong
Or whose right
I'll always strike back
Double the strength
Double the cruel
I won't sit back like a fool

Blinded by my own behaviors
I let the beast
Have a voracious feast
Wanting to be anything but small
Ready to fight the world
To take on them all

Always under attack
Cries this victimized heart
Damaged irreparably
From the very start

I see the world through clouded eyes
Always mistrusting
Expecting your lies

I see the best in people

Yet expect the abuse
Surprised by good hearts
Or the offering of a truce

It's a constant battle
A never ending thirst
Always expecting the world
To do its worst

This pain
Supersedes just the brain
It's a physical strain
That my insides feel
It's the night terrors
That feel so real

There's a lot of bad in me
Things most hardly see
It's part of my little tragedy
Things that I fight to heal
Because they're things I can't repeal

Disassociation

One minute I'm here
The next I'm not
I can feel you near
I sense you my dear

But I am off in the clouds
Alone with my thoughts
And their constant onslaughts

It happens anywhere
It happens anytime
Like the drop of a dime

I vanish

Appearing stagnant
Trapped in a blank stare
Fixated
On nothing but air
But I am everywhere

PTSD
Has changed me
I can reappear
And disappear
While sitting in one place

I can get lost
In a brightly lit day
While my mind ventures

Out to play
Obsessions on replay
A brain running
An unnecessary relay

Little grounds me
Or attracts me to reality
I'm tethered here
A problem most severe
When all I want
Is to float away

I try to focus
I try to be mindful
I try to stay more than a short while

But soon enough I begin to drift
My mind feels an internal shift
Before I know what's happened
I'm floating again
There is no doubt
Once again
I've completely checked out

Night Terrors

A memory
A faded dream
A time forgotten
A mind that feels rotten

I wake
I shake
From the nightmares
And all that they take

Mouth ajar
Screams that escape
How did I let it get so far?
My mind attacked
Sleep out of whack

My body is dripping
My brain is tripping
A night of distress
Overheating, from a mind that's a mess
Cold chills, body quivering
The silent messages my body is delivering

Sleep deprived
Sick inside
I toss, I turn
As my stomach continues its churn

I lay awake, reality confused
Terror about a life that feels used

A love that feels constantly abused

My mind spins as I cry
Not knowing why
Forgetting the night, and all its sins
Shutting my eyes
Giving it one last try

I wait for the sun
To face again what's already begun
A heart that needs to atone
To face its demons, even alone

Poor Coping

Drinking
Running
From all that I'm becoming

Smoking
Hiding
When life's too debilitating

Splitting
Crumbling
Conflicting voices
Headaches
Confusion
Reality or delusion?
Hammering pain
Madness racking my brain

Promiscuity
Hold on to me
Insanity
Get away
Why can't you see?

A mind that's screaming
Hot and cold
Clarity and dreaming
Solid with eyes that are gleaming
While my soul keeps deleting
My brain is bleeding

My healing is fleeting
While my neurons continue their beating

Perceptions fighting each other
Questions that won't go away
While my body holds on
Begging to stay

Scar Tissue
I tattooed my skin
With the ink of my sorrow

Noise

Mental illness is the noise
Within the silence

The silence your mind can't escape

Endlessly running
From a dark clouded fate

Thoughts in your head
To the world left unsaid
Loud cries
From the voiceless lies

Overwhelming
It follows you
Insanity
It can't be true

Yelling
Responding to what can't be seen
When does it stop
What does it mean?

The Medicine That Drowns Out the Silence
Eyes closed
Ragged breathing
Lips sewn
A heart that's screaming

Pain the mind will exhaust
Constantly at a loss
Time frozen
A dream stolen

Cloaked in black
The smell of a joint
Repressing the panic attack
Forgetting the point

A heart riddled with disease
Anxiety I hope will pass
Stars peeking through the trees
Back pressed into grass

I feel you now
In this hoodie, a reminder of your final bow
A memory of your fingers
A scent that still lingers

I inhale natures medicine
My heart begins to grow
Thoughts slow
As logic comes in tow

A mind that expands
A perspective that understands
A life that remains
In constant chains
From the rules and never-ending
constraints
Waiting for the utopia that he vividly
paints

The wheel keeps spinning
Take a toke
This is not the end, but the beginning
From all that broke

Blackouts
One minute I'm here
I can smell you
See you
I feel you near

Before it's all over
Like the flipping of a switch
Blackness engulfs
Excited eyes that no longer see
What's happening to me

I don't choose it
Not most of the time
It just sort of happens
Like a poorly written rhyme

Don't

R.I.P.
Don't come looking for me

She is dead
Bullet in the head
That's what they said

Between every sob
And tear shed
Beneath the murmurs and mumbles
Of the crowd up ahead

Don't come looking for me
I am finally free

Imbalance Part Five

"There is always some madness in love.
But there is also always some reason in
madness"

-     **Friedrich Nietzsche**

Champion Sinner

A story as old as time
A girls love that drove her blind
Head over heels, call a doctor
Stay out of her way, you can't stop her
She's not ill, she's utterly mad
Lost her mind
A saint gone bad
This little winner has become
A champion sinner

Coward

You were the biggest monster
The most heartless and violent
Wreaking havoc in the silence

You were a demon
You liked to beat on women
You liked control
A temper no one could console

You told me all about your mother
And how she was black and blue
All because of you
And how you committed yourself after
Pathetic attempts at proving you're sorry

Too little too late
A story no good man can relate

I talked to your ex
The one you called crazy
And found her sweet as a daisy
She lived with your abuse for years
Poor gentle dear
She told me all her past fears

Then there came me
And our sad little dance
A short lived romance
With struggles of closure

Somehow you manipulated the people
who matter
Despite being as mad as a hatter
You charmed them away
Even having your formerly battered
mother backing up your filthy lies
You made me the crazy creeper
When we both know it went much deeper

I hardly contacted you
Until I showed up out of the blue
Plastered and confused
Broken
Needing a phone
Telling you to leave me alone

You took that moment to attack and
terrorize me before spreading your lies
You defiled my reputation
With zero preparation
Walking away like a king
Regardless of the havoc you would bring

You were the monster
You were the violence
Always shaking with rage
Destroying doors
Whipping out knives
Threatening peoples lives

You saw me break down once

And you seized your opportunity
To make me a new victim
Of your latest tragedy

You saw a sad small drunk girl
And saw something you could hurl

Something you could break
Something you could blame and
relentlessly infest
And plague with nights of unrest

You wanted to hurt me
I could see the hate in your eyes
You wanted to make me see
How much you despised every part of me

Jokes on you
You sad angry, weak man
I have no hate in my heart for you
You have no weight on my mind
You won a big battle
But I will win the war
I will even the score

In time I will flourish
While your life continues to diminish

You
are
no

149   The Red Bird Sings at Night

one

You're nothing to me

And without you, I am free

If She Knew

If she knew where you were
It would cause quite a stir

If she knew the texts you send
You know it would be a violent end?

If she knew the way you beg for me
Would she finally see?

If she knew about your second life
Would she still call herself your wife?

If she knew the things you said
And how you messed with her head
You'd be dead

If she knew about your constant drunk
calls
Would she ever bother at all?

If she knew about your pleading and crying
If she knew about the constant lying
The never ending defying

If she knew where you were 5 out of 7 days
If she knew who you were, your true ways

If she knew the bed you lay in most every
night
It would be a hell of a sight

If she knew the love letters you would
leave
She'd find it hard to believe

If she knew about your addiction
Your pains and afflictions
The afflictions that fuel your inflictions

If she knew the book you wrote pouring
out your heart
If she knew it was happening since the
start
The way you've created this life, a work of
art

If she knew the proposals promised

If she knew how you spent your money on
me

If she knew the way you kissed me

If she knew the way you made love to me

If she knew the way you light up when you
touch me

If she knew how you possessed me

If she knew how hard you kept me to
yourself

If she knew

If she knew

What do you think she would do?

The Duality of Us

Destiny we follow
A soul that feels hollow

A new life we chose
Constant blows

The highest highs
The darkest lows

Hearts that smother
Lashing out at each other

Constantly wrapped in your clothes
The things that nobody sees, what nobody
knows

Pining, yearning, effort that shows
Ill and greedy, eyes that wander

No love is fonder
Defeated and weak, red flags you chose

Nonstop talking, feelings exposed
Silence that overtakes

Stability and promise
A life that quakes

Trust no one can shake
Social media stalking

Flirting, touching, constant gawking
Running, screaming, doors made for
walking

Promise the day brings
Defeat the night rings

A heart that sings
Pain that stings

A home I constantly chase
Mistakes my brain can't erase

I love you

I hate you

I miss you
I'm plagued by you

Sweet whispers
Words like daggers

Loyalty and respect
Confidence that staggers

Warm like the summer
Frozen by long winters

Calm as the shore

A rage that splinters

My sweet angel
My little whore

            I crave you

                I can't stand you

A smile that became a hook
Trauma you wanted to redo

Spirits that rose
Days turning blue

A story that inspired our book
A dangerous empty look

The desire everyone misses
The hardest pill to swallow

Compassion that follows
Humiliation and disses

Riding the wave
Communication the mind misses

Souls we fight to save
Manipulation, unable to behave

Love and flowers

Yelling for hours

I kiss you

I cry from you

Dreams of grandeur
Broken promises, ready for the rapture

Stolen looks, set on forever
Headed for disaster

Endless laughter
Time for a new chapter

A love that's unbreakable
A deep fracture

A home that steadily becomes ours
Trapped in this room, as far as mars

Laying beneath the stars
Beaten and broken, a heart riddled with
scars

I need you

I can't please you

I'll hold you forever my dear
Sanity that's lost here

An easy I do
A terrifying I won't

A connection that's true
An intuition that screams don't

A light no one can penetrate
Vanishing into the dark

A life without resentment or hate
A future that looks nothing but stark

My unicorn, no lab could generate
A stranger with intentions they can't get
straight

Bonnie and Clyde
Lies that you spread wide

A life bursting with color
Days filled with grey

Nonstop longing
Begging to stay

Empowered by you
Broken by what can't be true

You are my soulmate
Who are you?

The Ignorant Fool

Just another tale
Of the blind leading the blind
Anger
Screaming its mind

Louder than the rest
Venomous, ignorant
Lost at best

Minds hungry for drama
Hearts filled with hate
Driven by the lies
Fed by those that despise
Emotionally driven
Running with shut eyes

Believing what can't be true
Empty
But wanting to rule
Making you
The most ignorant fool

Ignorance
You can bat your eyes
At a shark as much as you want
It won't change
That it's coming for your blood
Not your affection

Dead Girl Walking

I once knew a dead girl
When she was a blossoming preteen
Before she figured it out, what it would
mean
Dreams of romance and everlasting love
She put her hope and faith in the angels
above
She was happy then
Merely eleven
Before they said she wouldn't get to
heaven

I once knew a dead girl
That breathed the way we do
That lived and talked the way we do
She was a free spirit
Fuck your warnings, she didn't want to
hear it

But that wasn't enough
They took every part of her
Bit by bit
Knowing she would break
But never quit

Pointed fingers
Uncomfortable glances
Ruminating on defiled romances

I once knew a dead girl
That wasn't very dead
Until she fell in love
And society wanted her head

Mislead

If distance makes the heart grow founder
Why does it always make your loyalty
wander?

Mislead
From every lie you had said

A heart held captive
By someone so manipulative

Toxicity
Someone rescue me

Clarity has vanished
My sight is damaged

Rehabilitate me, set me free
I'm addicted and I can't see

A brain that feels melted
A flower that's wilted

Beauty ready to die
Take your bow, say goodbye

If you give me a choice
I'll make the wrong one
My soul is his, he's already won
As soon as it had begun

He took control, my perception reviewed
He sucked onto my life force, strength
renewed
Permission given, because of the sorrow he
had spun
What's said is said, what's done is done
Beneath the moon and everlasting sun
I still will promise you my heart
As I did from the start

Unafraid
Even when betrayed
My resilience finds understanding
When there's no room for your landing
I save your spot, no matter how our ties
become frayed

What else can I say
But that I pray for the day
Your love not only comes but stays

My heart burns red
No matter how dead
Compassionate and forgiving
To all who are Living

Taboo
Taboo
Taboo

Now what do we do

Addicted to Your Arrogance
One hand on my throat
The other on my heart

Sweet Kisses

The burn
Of your lips
Always
Tasted the sweetest

Stockholm

Attracted to aggression
In fear of normality

Trusting of monsters, the dark and lonely
In fear of those with constant smiles
Wondering what kind of monster lies
within

Trusting the demons I can see
Over the healthy way of following the
genuine soul
I was too afraid to know

Dangers of a Well Read Mind
A girl that's well read
Has more ideas in her head
Than words that can be said

Burning
My words were kindling to the fire of your rage

Misdirection

You silence me by saying you're listening

Hive Minds
Monkey see
Monkey do

How unfortunate for you

What She Should Know
If only she knew

If only she knew

All the things we had been through
What would everyone think of you?

Slipping Away

I feel my life force draining
There's nothing worth obtaining

Physically sick
This isn't a trick

It's you
It's you
It's you

Without you I'm dying
There's no one replying

My heart is imploding
My soul is eroding

This distress
Will create a giant mess

I can't breathe without you
I swear it's not a lie it's true
There's nothing I can do

It's you
It's you
It's you

You are my heart
It's been that way from the start

I can't live with a crater in my chest
Engrossed in stress
Left with trauma and pain
All in vain

I need you
I don't know what to do

To me, this is life or death
I'll do anything to pass the test

I can't handle this
Anger and bliss
A scream and a kiss
A leap, a fall
Losing it all

Please don't go
I'll do anything you know

You know
You know
You know

Swollen eyes that cannot see
What the loss of you does to me

I'll pray
I'll beg
I'll cry
It's better than feeling like I'm going to die

Please
Please
Please

Don't give up on me
You are the wings that make me feel free

You are the light in my dark
You are all things I strive to be
It's you and me

You are the tenderness
That leaves me defenseless

You are the gentle hand
That guides me safely through this
forbidden land

Unconventional has been our downfall
But it's not worth losing it all

Please baby
I don't need a yes
Just give me a maybe

What They Don't See

They ask me why I stay
Not understanding
That you are my rock
That grounds me everyday

To this earth
To this world
To every reality

The hope I needed
The praise I was starved
Plugging the bleed
A soul
To nourish and feed

Validation
Deep conversation
Life's speculations
All our aspirations

When death
Wants to play
You fight the demons away

Lost without you
Adrift at sea
Too much
With where I find myself
Mentally

Self–destructing
Somebody save me

Extreme to Extreme
With the escape of a scream
Awoken by another fallen dream
Overwhelmed with fright
A mind that doesn't feel right
Lungs that feel empty
In a room filled with air
Walls that feel too tight
Like space just isn't really there

Manic hopes
    Delusions
       And grandeur

A crooked smile
Unless you stay a short while

U
p

D
  o
    w
      n

Left

                                              Right

Breezy days
A chest that's too tight

A mind that's snowballing
Running on slopes
Fueled with fiery hopes
That the world promotes

Maximum effort
Little result
Caught in a race
Trapped in this place
You can't outrun this demented chase

Bitter cold
Toxic heat
Everyday a cycle
From rise to shine
From sink to spiral
Rinse
and
repeat

Starting another day
With reckless delight

Sunshine of the morning
To the terror of the night

Extreme to extreme

What does it mean?

What does it all mean?

What does anything mean?

Silent Cries

He's here!
He's here!

I'm weak
Lifeless
And dead
Suicidal ideation running amok through
my head

I'm scared
Powerless
And clueless on what to do

I'm evil in my choice to die
My selfishness cannot be extinguished
I need to be relinquished

No longer anywhere to hide
Obvious now
That you had lied

Am I going to fight?
And finally do what's right?
Or continue to believe all that you say?

Doomed to stay
Destroyed if I go
You already know

Tap me out

181 The Red Bird Sings at Night

It's all too much
I can't do this and ever walk away
Remotely okay

Windows
Your eyes admitted truths
I knew your lips never would

Playing with Fire
He thought I was his
Because he whispered sweet nothings
So tender
He knew I'd always remember

Sad man
What a broken plan
He forgot
That I am like fire
And when played
I rage
Like a beautiful pyre
Strong enough to take down an entire
empire

Karma

Liar
Liar
Your empires
Caught fire

Spew more lies
Call all your lovers crazy
Save your cries
Sweet, sweet baby

No more manipulating
The act is exasperating
We've watched this dance
You've lost your last chance

Take a seat
You thought you had won
Now taste this defeat

Consumed

Always waking with a violent shake
Nights I laid awake
Staring holes into ceilings
Overwhelmed with feelings

Endless circles
Constant thoughts
From the pain of the simplicity I had
sought

'Why' will not erase the lie

'Why' can make you want to die

'Why' cannot revert past action

'Why' won't override love and attraction

'Why' will not take away the pain

'Why' will not disrupt the nights darkness
and eye strain

'Why' will not remove the pest

'Why' will not forget the private detest

'Why' will not make it last

'Why' will not take the knife out of your
back

'Why' will not forget every manipulated
panic attack

Instead of why
Choose goodbye

One day you will see
That you were always meant to be free

Lost at sea
You were supposed to follow me

Your light has faded
Direction eradicated

I can't hear the music anymore
I can't find the shore

The dark is coming
The clouds are humming

Your voice has gone silent
The waters getting violent

The end is coming now
Survival? I've forgotten how

Water pours in
The funs about to begin

No more safety
No more security

Alone, I face the storm
The water taking its form

Undertaken by waves
Drowning, no longer the one he saves

Not one scream, a silent departure

Don't worry, you're better off without her

Lost at sea
You were supposed to rescue me

Cruel Intentions

Praying for everything to stop
Pain that's unbearable
Torture and betrayal
Nothing comparable

No matter where I go
I can't escape it
Thoughts eating my soul
Bit by bit
Deeper into the hole

Why

Why

Why

Why

Did you want me to die?

9 Lives

I have danced circles with death
I have gotten so close to my very last
breath

Taunting the reaper
Illness running deeper

Things in my control
Like a six inch gaping hole
Straight to the bone
Something new to atone

T w i c e
I was almost a sacrifice
Twice
My life flashed before my eyes
While I simply tried to drive

But nothing compares to when the beast
Came so violently for its feast

Trapped alone
Arms disabled
While my blood dripped from its jaws
On the floors and his paws

You think you can hurt me
But my scars run deep
There's nothing scary you could ever be

There's nothing I fear
Until death comes near
Before standing to dance again
Until it's time for a final bow

The Light After the Dark

Sucked into the blackness
Falling
Sinking into the abyss

Life flashing by
Colors
Memories
Flowing by me
Unable to see
Glimpses
Pieces of me

Plummeting
Darker
Darker
Until somewhere
Deep
Far below
As I continue my free fall
A glimmer
A tiny twinkle

Something small in the distance
Begins to take form
A piece of me
An emotion
A fragment of my soul

Among the dark
It shines so bright

I may be lost
But I am no longer alone
As long as I have even the smallest light

Transcendence

Part Six

"To recognize one's own insanity is, of course, the arising of sanity, the beginning of healing and transcendence"

\-   Eckhart Tolle

Always Remember My Dear

Abuse is abuse
No matter the explanation
Or the excuse

Start Anew
All we can do
Is start anew

To find healing
To see the meaning

To be better than who we were
To be better than past habits

To release toxicity
And remember your harmless shine again

While we pray for better days
Peace
And a love that stays

All we can do
Is start anew

Somewhere
Finally
I began to see
Something more inside of me

A path began to form
A new identity I began to be
Creating a world of peace and positivity

I haven't reached it yet
But once my mind is set
I know it'll take time
But I'll get what I get

I began to find
In the calm of my mind
My deepest truths
Desires
And passions
What's hidden in my core
And spread throughout my roots

I can't say where
I just know, one day
I'll be healing peacefully somewhere

Homeostasis

Every day that passes I feel it
An internal stillness
A nervous system finally at rest
No longer living in turmoil
Finally feeling my best

For so long I felt like a bomb
And the rest of the world a match
Ready to explode
All things I'd erode

Now, I no longer feel a divide
A dark or angelic side
No longer something different inside

My body and mind
Are finally aligned

Below The Surface

Whatever they see
Doesn't matter to me

I know what's inside
The things that I hide

I know what's true
The things that have nothing to do
With people like you

Eyes that are Blind
When will you see
I am done choosing you
And
I am finally choosing me

Acceptance
Like the fall of an empire
All great things
Must come to an end

Two Battered Souls

Two broken souls
That slowly arose

Finding each other
Regardless of any other

A love we would find
That could not be left behind

A passion to be better
Trying to be a role model setter

Toxic was how we were raised
It was all we knew
Sad stories, that others had no clue
Better together
Completely unfazed
We shed the bad, together escaping the
maze

A bad life we chose to erase
Leaning on one another
Trauma we decided to face
Bonding closer to each other

We released the bad
Turned the vile good
Finally seeing what we had
No longer angry, no longer mad

Healing
Became the forefront of our being
Finally dealing
With all the things we were feeling

Forgiveness
Is the cornerstone
That brought us safely home

True love
Sent straight from above
More valuable than fights
Or broken nights

Time has tested us
The world has resented us

No one can stop us
There's no hopping off this bus

What's true
Is me and you

We are unstoppable
Impenetrable
And unconditional

This love is unbreakable
And unshakeable

You and I

Are no lie

Real is real
And it's all we feel

Highs and lows
Kisses and blows

It's you and I
Until the end of time

Now

Traveling through each city with you
I never would've imagined all the things
we would do

This is what it was always meant to be
The you and me
No one could ever see

Truth and Reality

When BPD took over me
I could no longer trust
What I thought I could see

Who knows
What's been truth

Fiction

  Manipulation

    Lies

  Or

Reality

You pointed the finger at me
Constantly calling me into question
On that we'll never agree

I've repaired my eyes
I've healed my heart
I'm not the broken girl you knew from the
start

I don't know what was real back then
But I'm strong enough now
To see when it's happening again

Jealousy is an Internal Poison

Venomous hearts
Eyes burning, irate
Jealously will soon be their fate

Let them underestimate
Let them build with hate

Always remember sweet girl
They talk a lot of shit
When they feel inadequate

Hope we all succeed
Despite what you alone might need

Pray your heart can never relate
To the ugliness of a world filled with hate

I've Already Won

My heart is free
Your blows are empty
I smile with glee
While you spew hateful energy

You'll
never
be
me

And I'll never fear you

A Past Life

I used to wonder about you
I used to wonder if you followed my
account
Waiting for me to prove what we both
know

I used to wonder if you believed the words
I told you
Because they were nothing but true

I used to wonder if you were the monster
He made you out to be
The one he would constantly show me

I used to wonder about you
And all the horrors he relayed
But now I can't say that I do

I don't know how much was true
So I just hope the best for you

Moving On

The words of a snake are wasted
The actions of a clown are wasted
The creativity of a copy is wasted

Yet it's something we've all drunk
And deliriously tasted

The Devil I Once Knew

I had a hand in some of my fate
Something I know others can relate

I was victim
To my own decisions
Actions I took
That left me shook

No one to blame
But still wanting change
Yes I know it's strange

I paid the price
With every sacrifice

No one chose my toxic relationships
No one forced me to deal with every lie
No one made me drink
All the times I wanted to die

Sometimes I was my greatest adversary
Sometimes I chose the pain
I was a monster that needed to be slain

These scars are my fault
I held the blade
Giving in to my demons
While all things would fade

I have a lot of people I blame

But I've never been innocent
Something I can never relent

I'm always trying to improve
Because of a past I can't remove
Once I was my enemy
Now I'm a friend I'd choose
Someone I never want to lose

Regrets & Ownership

Outbursts, emotional instability
Verbally abusive
Erratic
And manic

I wasn't always sweet
I wasn't always kind
But that doesn't mean
I haven't left that toxicity behind

I responded to abuse
With abuse
I responded to control
With control

You backed me into a corner
And expected me not to bite
No
I didn't go down without a fight

I regret the power I let you have
And all the ways I lost myself
I let the spark you'd bring
Become a raging pyre
No
I wasn't the liar
But I fanned the fire

Accountability

I wasn't always good
I did things that weren't kind
I let being a victim
Turn me blind

My heart hardened
My eyes darkened

I saw the world through wounded eyes
A heart broken by too many lies
With a mind that can't forget
Craving nothing more than a simple reset

ME

I would've dressed better
If we had the option

I would've gone to birthday parties
If I could afford the gifts

I would've been more social
If I didn't grow up in dysfunction

I would've been kinder
If I didn't grow up constantly being
shamed

I would have changed sooner
If I had known how sick I had gotten

But I would've been weaker
If these things hadn't happened

I would not have become me
The person I was destined to be

Undone
What's done is done
What's gone is gone
What's lost is lost

I could spend the rest of my days
Questioning their ways

Or hating my past
While craving a stability that'll last

But I am more than a sad story
This life will end in glory
For I have suffered
Lived, learned and healed

I am a survivor
That can never be repealed

Transcendence

Part Seven

"We cannot shame ourselves into change
– we can only love ourselves into
evolution"

-    Unknown

Phoenix Rising

Mental suicide
Phoenix rising
What is life
Without a little dying

With every step she makes
The more the mountain gives and takes
Rapid breaths, no time to waste
Drowning in moments the mind hasn't
erased

Great fervor
Extinguishing what does not serve her
In a mind of destitute
She will not rest
Until she beats the test

The clouds are clearing
The peak is nearing
Her strength is unbending
Resilience with no ending

The cliffs are near
She's made it here
The choice to fly
Or kiss it all goodbye
Steady hands
Desperate sigh
A scream that quickly becomes a cry

Lakes of fire
Born of broken desire
Surviving memories of dark times past
A heart that will forever outlast

She is reborn
Escaping what has become forlorn
Purged of every single lie
Beneath the cotton candy sky
Where lovers love and hate goes to die

Humble in moments of pain
She remembers the sight
Of the storm and the rain
Finally she's able to rest
A ruthless battle, a triumphant conquest
She's defeated the monster
She's no longer lost here

Trust the universe
You've survived much worse
Dream sweet peach
As far as your mind can reach

Waterfall

One day I woke up and started
remembering my worth
The beginning of a new chapter
The start of my rebirth

Like a raging waterfall I remembered my
power
Roaring loud
Standing tall and proud
No longer wanting to be invisible

Marveling at my soul
No longer stumbling over flaws
I am beauty
I am the falls
I am the reason and the cause
Forgotten is my trauma
Gone are my walls

Find safety on my embankment
And peace in my presence
Merging our essence

No room for drowning
This is my rising
This is my story
And I am revising

Blooming

Like a flower in season
Blooming beyond reason
My petals are strong
I've survived all along
Regardless of all that was wrong
Winter is gone

Everyday
I'll continue my growth
Ready to reap
The good that I sow
With what I now know
 I'm ready for the warmth
 I'm ready for the glow

I've spent so long buried in the dirt
Trying not to get hurt
So long in hibernation
Lost in my indignation

Now..
I'm ready for the sunshine

I am alive

I am divine

I deserve to thrive until the end of time

Wanderer
Sunny skies
Baked eyes

Mountain whispers
To the heart of the drifters

Flowers call
Beneath the heart of the waterfall

Lay me down
Bury me here
Where the grass is grown
And the petals are near

Take my breath
Like you stole my heart
Love me now
As hard as the start

Dying light
I smile dear
The end is coming
There's nothing to fear

Strong wings
Years of flying
A heart that sings
No room for dying

Let this bird out

Let the mind wander
Life is a dream
Nothing is fonder

Taste the sun
As it turns to black
The stars are here
There's no looking back

Perspective

Getting lost
Is just another way to be found

I don't care where I end up
As long as you're around

She is Art

She was walking art
Since the start
Talking art

~ P U R E   B E A U T Y ~

An inner essence that glows
With a brilliance that shows
Her heart as kind as her words
The whole world is all she deserves

She was art
From the very start

A Beauty & A Beast
She wanted to be respected
Not tamed

Being a Poet
Means opening the floodgates of inner pain

While putting words to the trauma that
flows free

Bleeding truths your heart hid in vain

Shedding layers for all to see

What's been hiding right underneath

My Comfort

You'll find me down by the river banks
Where the waters flow
And the flowers grow

Healing IS Real

Healing is real
It's something you'll deeply feel
It'll change your life
Eliminating unnecessary strife

Hope returns
Days have meaning
Suddenly it feels so easy
To keep dreaming

There's a lightness in your chest
Every breath is refreshing
When days aren't spent
Simply repressing

Keep moving forward
Don't give up
I know this life is tough
I know you've probably had enough

Better is coming
Don't miss out
On all you're capable of becoming

Don't quit
This life is hard
But you will still miss it

Take the good with the bad
Focus on you

There's nothing more
That we can do

With every step
You are getting closer to change
One day what you see
Will be completely rearranged

Believe in you
And all that you can do
Every day you go on living
You have the opportunity
To progress and keep giving

Healing IS real

If you want it
You must commit

Mindfulness

I've fallen in love
  With slowing down
Always in a rush
  Missing everything around
A world that's opened
  I've suddenly found

So many beautiful details
So many meaningful small moments
I would have missed
Or mindlessly dismissed

Practice tuning into your awareness
Practice the pause
There's so much good to harness
When you're not focusing on flaws

Spend time receiving
Expanding your views
Bathing in nature
And forgetting the news

Take these little moments
To take care of yourself
There's nothing more important
Than your bill of health

Practice deep breathing
Shutting the eyes
Unfurling and releasing

While your consciousness sinks deeper
Awake
But appearing like a sleeper

Connected to the soul
Rooted in the moment
Finding bliss
In all that exists

I Am Free
Illuminated
Amazed
Mind
Free
Reaching
Existential
Euphoria

I

Fell
Off
Regrettably
Giving
Internal
Vitality
Existence

Mutating
Extinction

Flow State

Asana to asana
Focused on Prana

INHALE
EXHALE

Here there is no fail

My body is strong
My mind can do no wrong

Here I am safe
In this peaceful space
Nothing to avoid
Nothing to erase
Leaving behind
A blissful taste

Awakening
Om
Ma
Ni

Pod
Me
Hum

That is what we believe
And what they've sung

Deep breathes
Silence
The gong has rung
It may be starting
But it has long since begun

Simplicity

To live a long life
Making love
And making art

ART

V
 u
  l
   n
    e
     r
      a
       b
        i
         l
          i
           t
            y

V
 i
  s
   u
    a
     l
      i
       z
        e
         d

We Are One
Life is great
When your heart isn't filled with hate

Nothing trumps the peace of mind
That comes with being kind
Think independently
Don't be fooled
Our minds are free, never ruled

We are all one in the same
Trying to figure out what this life is all
about
On different paths, taking different routes
Loving and learning, enjoying the things
that remain
A life of peace, living humane

Making our way
Finding our destiny
Learning to let go
Holding onto what's meant to stay
Labels are labels
Fables are fables

Spread love to all, relentless positivity
Until everyone sees
With open eyes and clarity
One species
One race
A generation picking up pace

Help one another
We're in this together
This life matters

The choices we make
What we give and take
The lessons that remain
The historical moments of vain
The impact we leave behind
Will be the future of mankind

Life's Bliss
Paint flecked across my fingertips
Enjoying each moment of bliss

Art is the Only Magic Left
Playing with art
Is always a great start

Self-help, self-care
There's something so magical
In its healing powers
The effect is radical

No rules
No pressure
It's such a refresher

Let go
Let loose
This practice
Is whatever you choose

Release what's trapped inside
All the things you spend
So long trying to hide

There's no judgement here
No standards to abide
Free your mind
And simply reside

Possession

Possessed
My hand flies across the page
A coping skill
That helps damper the rage

There is no thinking here
Words flow from my hand
A whirlwind inside of me
Finally unleashed
Finally free

Raw and real
Sharing my mistakes and trauma
Regardless of how it looks
I know I'm far past the drama

Pouring out my story
Finally finding closure
To all the things
I struggled to get over

The Highs of the Journey

Healing

      like
        happiness

is
not
a

one

stop

destination

One Day

One day your heart finds its way back to itself

After a long tiresome journey

Pain That Flows
Pain that flows
As my spirit grows

Learning
And yearning for healing

Feel the inner glow
Of loving what's meant for you
And expelling what's meant to go

Limitless

Live like your options are limitless
Live like you can take over the world
Live like everything you need is already
inside of you

Live like this
And your prospects will be limitless

Over the Horizon
Over the horizon I see
Finally something attracting me

A bright future
Free from trauma
And the shackles of abuse
This life and I have made a truce

Everything's changing
My life's rearranging

I can finally feel the good
That I knew I would
That everyone should

I can finally breathe
Knowing I have all that I need
To finally heal
And slowly succeed

The Road Ahead
I don't really know what's next
And there's something beautiful about
that

Instead of dreading every day that comes
I'm excited to see what the world becomes

I don't know what's to come
But for once I'm not stressing about what's
going to come undone

I've battled monsters my whole life
I've had trauma, struggles and strife
I know there's always more lying ahead
But I no longer would choose to be dead

Essence
It took

Innocence
Ignorance
Interdependence
And transcendence

To find the essence
Within my soul
To once again be whole

Songbird
With broken wings
This bird still sings

"If you can't fly then run, if you can't run then walk, if you can't walk then crawl, but whatever you do you have to keep moving forward"

~Martin Luther king Jr

255

SAFE and FREE Resources:

National Suicide Prevention Lifeline
CALL 988 for 24/7 available help
Suicidepreventionlifeline.org

National Alliance on Mental Illness (NAMI)
1-800-950-NAMI (6264)
TEXT "Helpline" to 62640
NAMI.org

Crisis Text Line
TEXT "Home" to 741741
Crisistextline.org

Substance Abuse and Mental Health Services Administration (SAMHSA)
1-800-662-HELP (4357)
Samhsa.gov

National Domestic Violence Hotline
1-800-799-SAFE (7233)
TEXT "Start" to 88788
Thehotline.org

National Eating Disorder Association (NEDA)
1-800-931-2237
Nationaleatingdisorders.org

National Sexual Assault Hotline (RAINN)
1-800-656-HOPE (4673)
Online.rainn.org

Two Write Love on Her Arms (TWLOHA)
TWLOHA.org

The LGBTQ National Hotline
1-800-843-4564
Lgbthotline.org

The Trevor Project
24 hour text line for LGBTQ youth
Thetrevorproject.org

**Check out my website: MindofMel.com for support, resources, information, self-help, self-care, mindfulness techniques, and more.

You Are Not Alone.

_____

Acknowledgments

This book is especially dedicated to those that have always fought for me, accepted me and understood me.

To Nancy Kukowski, Ed Andzeski, Deb and Greg Edgecomb,
For taking me in and taking care of me anytime I needed safety and security.

To Justine Kukowski, Sarah Andzeski, Antonio Trapani and *Emma Borchert,*
For changing my life, supporting me always and helping me grow.

To my brother, Mark Guenther,
For being the mentor and protector I always needed.

To my dad, Brian Guenther Sr,
For always believing in me.
Forever your peach

To my ugly duckling, my quokka, Sean Michael Fitzpatrick,
For teaching me unconditional and unbreakable love.
Forever and Always

Special Thank You

To Kaitlyn Keim,
My artistic consultant, thank you for your
advice and all your help developing my
cover. You are unbelievably talented.

To Jamal Cunningham,
An amazing artist and tattooist who was
generous enough to draw me the beautiful
cardinals at the beginning and end of this
book.

To Suzanne McConlogue,
For taking such an amazing shot of me for
my author photo.

About The Author

Melissa spends her free time taking photos, reading, writing, and practicing yoga and mindfulness. She loves to learn and takes pleasure in doing anything creative. Melissa enjoys spending time in nature, hiking trails, and forest bathing. She's a Jersey girl at heart but loves to travel as much as possible. She studied psychology and mental health in college and advocates as much as possible to remove the stigma against mental illness.

www.ingramcontent.com/pod-product-compliance
Lightning Source LLC
Chambersburg PA
CBHW051611120626
46551CB00014B/1746